For a long time, scientists believed that some mammals (such as camels, giraffes, elephants, and pigs) couldn't swim at all. But now we realize that all the mammals we know of—even bats—can swim, though some do so only rarely or with difficulty.

Symphurus thermophilus is a species of tonguefish that inhabits hydrothermal vents near underwater volcanoes in the Pacific Ocean. They can withstand water that exceeds 100°C (212°F) in temperature.

There are around three million shipwrecks on ocean floors around the world. These include ancient galleys, ships from explorers, pirates, and merchants, and many naval ships. The seafloor is a true archaeological museum!

Lack of oxygen and natural light and a thick layer of silt (sand or clay grains) underwater help preserve ancient objects. Low salinity (salt content) and cold water, as in the Baltic Sea, protect books and clothes, even after several hundreds of years underwater.

water

DISCOVERING THE PRECIOUS RESOURCE ALL AROUND US

OLGA FADEEVA

TRANSLATED BY LENA TRAER

EERDMANS BOOKS FOR YOUNG READERS

GRAND RAPIDS, MICHIGAN

An entire world is reflected in a drop of water.

Does water make you wonder?

Once upon a time, about 4.6 billion years ago, our planet formed. And then, about 3.7 billion years ago, the first microscopic forms of life emerged. These microorganisms first appeared in the oceans that covered nearly every surface of the planet at that time, and then later started to colonize the atmosphere. Fungi were the first to leave the water and establish life on land, followed by plants and animals. Billions of years passed before humans appeared.

Ever since those ancient times, we've encountered water every single day. We drink water, and use it to bathe, brush our teeth, and wash our clothes. No living being—whether plant or animal—can survive without water. What is water, then, if not the most precious resource on our planet?

Did dinosaurs also see their reflection in the ancient raindrops?

How much water is there on Earth?

Only 29% of the Earth's surface is covered by land—the rest is covered by water. Most of the planet's water is salt water. Only a tiny fraction is fresh water, and most of that fresh water is either underground or frozen in glaciers. Only 1% of the world's fresh water is accessible for direct human use. We find that water in rivers, lakes, atmosphere, and soil.

71% of the Earth's surface is covered with water.

3% of the world's water is fresh water.

Only 1% of the world's fresh water is easily accessible.

Some of the largest reservoirs of fresh water in the world are located in Zambia and Zimbabwe, Russia, Ghana, and Canada.

Why does it rain?

Water is the only substance on Earth present in nature in three different states: solid, liquid, and gas. Ice and snow are forms of water. So are steam, clouds, and fog. Water is constantly moving and, it seems, can suddenly disappear and reappear. How does it work?

The sun heats up water in seas and oceans and through evaporation turns it into vapor or steam. Water vapor rises, mixes with cold air, cools, and condenses into a liquid form. These tiny water droplets cling together and form clouds. This is also how fog and dew form. When the droplets of water become heavy enough, they fall to the ground as rain. And if the air is really cold, they turn into snow or hail.

Air currents move clouds across huge distances, and rain often falls far from the place where clouds originally formed. Rain nourishes soil and replenishes groundwater, streams, and rivers—which bring water back to the seas and oceans. This is the never-ending water cycle.

The amount of water that evaporates each year is about the same as the amount of water delivered to the Earth as precipitation. That is why we don't run out of water.

Clouds trap heat on Earth, keeping it from cooling down.

what Do clouds Tell us About the weather?

Ice clouds, also called cirrus clouds, look like feathers, flakes, or white streamers high in the sky. Made up of ice crystals, they form at high altitudes where it is colder. Precipitation from these clouds evaporates before reaching the Earth's surface.

Stratus clouds appear as gray layers that cover the entire sky. They are composed of water droplets and ice crystals, and may produce a light drizzle or a steady rain.

Cumulus clouds look like airy white puffs. They most often form in the summer and don't produce rain.

Cumulonimbus clouds are very large, with a vertical height of several kilometers (or miles). We usually call them storm clouds. They can bring heavy rain, thunderstorms, lightning, and hail.

Clouds only seem to be weightless. Even a small cloud can weigh several tons, because it is made up of many water droplets.

Plants and animals are also part of the water cycle whenever they move water or consume it.

IS there water underground?

It's hard to imagine that under our feet, deep underground, there is a vast reservoir of water. We call this groundwater.

Subsoil waters are located immediately below the surface. They are constantly replenished by rains, melting snow, and nearby rivers and lakes, so their levels fluctuate.

Deeper underground, between impermeable layers of rock and clay (which don't allow liquids to pass through them), you will find confined water. The deepest layers of groundwater are artesian water and mineral water. These waters are under pressure, and sometimes they emerge through fissures and cracks in the ground to form springs at the Earth's surface. Rocks are a perfect natural filter, so artesian water is some of the cleanest on the planet.

SUBSOIL WATER

CONFINED WATER

ARTESIAN WATER

Some rivers begin high in the mountains, forming from glaciers and melting snow.

A SOURCE is the place where a river begins.

Other rivers form from SPRINGS, points where groundwater naturally emerges from underground.

How do rivers form?

A river is a large amount of water flowing continuously through a riverbed from its source to the mouth. Rivers can flow in any direction (north, south, east, or west), but they always flow downhill.

It's impossible to count how many rivers there are in the world. In China, there are over 1,500 rivers; in the United States, there are over 250,000 rivers. In Russia, there are over two million rivers—from the smallest streams to great rivers like the Yenisei, Ob, Irtysh, Amur, Lena, and Volga.

The Amazon River and the Nile are competing for the title of longest river in the world—it all depends on how you measure their lengths. The widest river is the Río de la Plata or River Plate (at its mouth). The Congo River is the deepest.

A RIVERBED is the ground which a river flows over.

When a river flows into another river, adding its water to the flow of the larger river, it is called a TRIBUTARY.

A RIVER MOUTH is the place where a river flows into a larger river, a lake, a sea, or an ocean. Sometimes, a river just dries up in the desert.

Sometimes, rivers are formed from water flowing out of lakes or bogs.

How are rainbows and water related?

A rainbow is an optical phenomenon that appears when sunlight is refracted, bending in water droplets.

Light from the sun appears white and transparent, but it's actually made up of lots of different colors of all wavelengths. Light rays are refracted and reflected in water droplets floating in the air. The larger the droplets, the brighter the rainbow. You can see a rainbow in the sky after rainfall, and in the spray from waterfalls, fountains, and geysers.

There are many different waterfalls on our planet: small streams and also large, powerful waterfalls with huge volumes of water. There are waterfalls that flow over cliffs in one wide wall, and waterfalls made up of many different streams of water cascading around rocks. And if sunlight hits these waterfalls just right, it brings a show of dazzling rainbows.

THE IGUAZÚ FALLS is the largest system of waterfalls in the world. It is located on the border of Argentina and Brazil.

THE KHONE FALLS is the world's widest waterfall. It is located in Laos near the border with Cambodia.

ANGEL FALLS in Venezuela is the highest waterfall in the world.

A WATERFALL is a place where water drops from a height, either over a sharp cliff or down some other type of incline.

A rainbow is always formed in a direction opposite to that of the sun.

In Iceland, water from geysers and hot springs is used for heating houses, greenhouses, and swimming pools.

GEYSERS are hot springs that erupt, sending jets of water and steam into the air.

Geysers are usually found in areas with volcanic activity. They may look like puddles of boiling water, or they can shoot water up to tens of meters high. The spray from these geysers is another great place to spot rainbows.

You can see geysers in Chile, Iceland, and the Kamchatka Peninsula of Russia. Yellowstone National Park in the US has more geysers than any other area of the world.

what are Lakes?

A lake is a body of water, entirely surrounded by land, that does not flow directly into a sea or an ocean. Lakes form in a number of different ways.

Some lakes were formed by the melting of glaciers.

Some lakes formed in old riverbeds . . .

Other lakes appeared as a result of tectonic movements of the Earth's crust.

. . . cracks in the bedrock . . .

. . . and even craters of dormant volcanoes.

LAKE BAIKAL is the deepest lake in the world. It holds more than 20% of the drinking water on our planet.

THE CASPIAN SEA is the largest lake in the world. It has historically been called a sea because of its large size, but it has only a third of the saltiness of most oceans and seas.

THE DEAD SEA is the most lifeless lake. It is so salty that only some microorganisms can survive in its water: algae, bacteria, and fungi.

LAKE SUPERIOR is the largest freshwater lake in the world. It is one of the five large lakes known as the Great Lakes, located on or near the Canada–United States border.

CANADA is considered the country with the most lakes. It is home to several million lakes, which formed over time because of the country's history of glaciers and its hard, rocky terrain—which water cannot seep through.

Some lakes form from springs, releasing water to the surface from deep underground.

Even Antarctica has lakes. They are covered by a layer of ice several kilometers thick. The largest of these subglacial lakes is Lake Vostok.

How is a sea different from an ocean?

BEAUFORT
SEA

BERING
SEA

BAFFIN
BAY

GULF OF
ALASKA

HUDSON
BAY

LABRADOR
SEA

Pacific
Ocean

North
America

SARGASSO
SEA

GULF OF
MEXICO

GULF OF
CALIFORNIA

CARIBBEAN
SEA

A sea is a smaller part of the global, interconnected ocean, that is partially enclosed by land or oceanic landforms.

There is still no consensus among scientists about exactly how many seas there are on Earth. Some say there are about 60 seas; others count more than 80. Some seas are in fact enormous salty lakes—like the Caspian Sea and the Dead Sea. And some gulfs—like the Persian Gulf or the Gulf of Mexico—are also considered seas.

No river can flow from the sea toward land, because sea level is below ground level and water always flows downward. But sometimes it's possible to see a river flowing into a sea that appears to flow backward. This happens occasionally during high tides or ice jams, or because of waves and strong winds from the sea.

How are the boundaries of a sea determined?

The main criteria are the salinity (saltiness) of the water, temperature, and natural obstacles such as islands, underwater ridges, rifts, and sometimes sea currents.

Every sea, just like every person, has its own character. Even two neighboring seas can have very different water temperature, depth of the seafloor, salinity, color, and frequency and size of waves. For example, the Greek island of Rhodes is washed by the calm and warm Mediterranean Sea on one side, and by the rough and cold Aegean Sea on the other side.

Sometimes seas meet, but their waters don't mix because of the difference in water temperature and salinity. There are a few places on our planet where you can see this happen—for example, where the Mediterranean Sea meets the Aegean Sea, or where the Baltic Sea and the North Sea meet.

SEA LEVEL
Global mean (average) sea level is the base level for measuring elevation and depth on Earth.

Atlantic Ocean

The Sargasso Sea, in the northwest part of the Atlantic Ocean, is sometimes called "the sea of sunken ships." Many ships were mired in its seaweed and unable to escape.

The Sargasso Sea is the largest sea on our planet. Located within the Atlantic Ocean, it is the only sea that has no land boundaries—its boundaries are defined by four ocean currents, together forming a clockwise-circulating system termed the North Atlantic Gyre. Because of this, the Sargasso Sea has a mean surface level approximately one meter higher than that of the surrounding waters. The currents also carry waste and seaweed, which they deposit into this sea, turning it into a vast, almost motionless "island." That's because there's often very little wind over the Sargasso Sea due to its position relative to the equator.

How is an ocean different from a sea?

An ocean is a large body of water that fills the space between continents. There are five main oceanic bodies of water.

THE PACIFIC OCEAN is the largest and the deepest of the world's ocean basins, representing about 30% of Earth's total surface area and nearly half of the planet's water surface area.

THE ATLANTIC OCEAN is the second-largest of the oceans, covering approximately 20% of Earth's surface. This is also the saltiest ocean.

Ocean water is constantly moving. The reason for this is waves and currents.

The biggest waves form in the open ocean. They are most commonly caused by the wind: the stronger it is and the longer it blows, the bigger the waves are going to be.

Ocean currents depend on wind, water temperature and salinity, tides, and the rotation of the Earth.

The global ocean conveyor belt

Both surface and deep-water ocean currents create what is known as the "global ocean conveyor belt": a constantly moving system, like an underwater river, that moves water through Earth's oceans. This system carries and mixes vast amounts of water, and also influences climate around the planet. As Earth warms from climate change, this system of currents will also be affected.

THE GLOBAL OCEAN
All the Earth's seas
and oceans.

TSUNAMIS are giant
waves usually caused by an
underwater earthquake.

Approaching the shore
as fast as a jet plane,
they rise to 30–50 meters
(98.4–164 feet) high and
crash onto the shore with
extreme power, destroying
many things in their way.
Most tsunamis occur in
the Pacific Ocean, where
earthquakes are common.

THE GULF STREAM
is one of the strongest and
warmest currents in the
northern part of the Atlantic
Ocean.

Originating in the tropics,
along the southern shores
of North America, it moves
northeast, flowing across
the Atlantic and bringing
warm waters to the shores of
western and northern Europe.
These vast masses of water
heat up the air, making the
climate of the coastal areas
near the Gulf Stream warmer
than the land farther from
the coast.

THE INDIAN OCEAN
is the third-largest of the world's five
oceans and is located entirely within
the Eastern Hemisphere.

THE ARCTIC OCEAN
is the coldest and shallowest of Earth's
oceans—and the smallest, only 1.5
times the size of the United States.

THE SOUTHERN OCEAN
surrounds Antarctica and is made up of
the portions of the world ocean south of
the Pacific, Atlantic, and Indian Oceans.

Why are the seas and the oceans salty?

Water in lakes can be salty, too. Two of the saltiest lakes in the world are Don Juan Pond in Antarctica and Gaet'ale Pond in Ethiopia—their salinity exceeds 400 grams of salt per liter (53 ounces of salt per gallon).

Scientists believe that seawater became salty due to volcanic activity millions of years ago. Gases released during volcanic eruptions reacted with seafloor rocks, making the water salty.

These days, rainwater washes the salt from rocks, and rivers carry it to the seas and oceans. Heat from the sun evaporates water while salt remains. More rainfall and more rivers flowing into the sea mean seawater that is more diluted by fresh water. That is why southern seas are saltier than seas in the north. Humans also add salt into our planet's water indirectly with the use of fertilizers, salt on icy roads, and water softeners.

The Red Sea is the saltiest sea in the world. No rivers flow into it, and due to the hot climate, water evaporates from it at a fast rate. Its salinity is 41 grams of salt per liter (5.5 ounces per gallon). The Baltic Sea has the lowest salinity of any sea—in some parts, it's only 2 grams of salt per liter (0.3 ounces per gallon).

On average, one liter of seawater contains 35 grams of salt; one gallon will contain about 4.5 ounces of salt. Besides water and salt, seawater consists of many other substances, including magnesium, calcium, potassium, and many others. That's why the taste of ocean water is different from drinking water, even when salt has been added to soften the water.

You can create beautiful textures in watercolor painting by sprinkling salt on top of your paint. This is the most saline illustration in this book.

Why are the seas and the oceans blue?

An artist needs all shades of blue to paint a sea: ultramarine, cobalt, cerulean, turquoise. Why does the sea look blue when water itself is transparent and colorless?

Turquoise

Cobalt

The color of the sea that we see depends on a number of factors, including how deep the sea is, how transparent the water is, the type and amount of minerals present, the color of the sky, and how many clouds there are. But primarily, it depends on how seawater absorbs and scatters light.

Sunlight contains the complete range of wavelengths of the electromagnetic spectrum. Long wavelength light—red—is absorbed more strongly by water: just a few meters deep, red objects will appear gray. Short wavelength light—blue—is absorbed less. That is why the blue rays penetrate to a deeper depth, and the sea appears blue.

Water in the sea may look green or even red due to the presence of microorganisms like algae.

Ultramarine

Cerulean

Indigo

Why don't rivers, especially shallow ones, appear as blue as the sea? What happens is that the current lifts sand, clay, and silt from the bottom of the river, and water becomes yellow, reddish brown, or grayish green. Rivers flowing from peat bogs may even look dark brown or black.

Who are the involuntary travelers in our oceans?

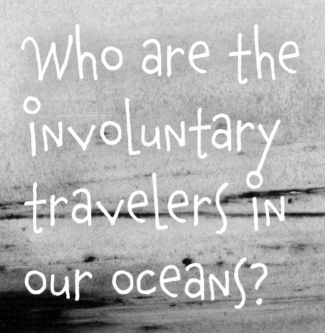

Icebergs are giant floating chunks of ice that have broken off from glaciers or ice sheets.

In the Northern Hemisphere, most icebergs are formed in Greenland and the Arctic Archipelago of Canada; in the Southern Hemisphere, most icebergs are formed in Antarctica and the Southern Patagonian Ice Field. Northern icebergs are smaller in size and mostly dome-shaped. Southern icebergs usually have steep sides and a flat top.

Some icebergs can be so big that they could fit a whole country. Such massive icebergs can travel around the ocean for more than ten years and drift far from where they formed.

About 90% of an iceberg is submerged beneath the surface, so you can only see the tip of the iceberg.

Some polar research stations are based on icebergs.

Icebergs cool the surrounding air, creating thick sea fog.

These floating ice mountains present a significant threat to ships, especially in the fog. Icebergs often appear like dark ghosts at a ship's front or side, and can do a great deal of damage if a ship hits one.

Because they come from glaciers or ice sheets, icebergs are also floating reserves of frozen fresh water. Scientists are studying ways to transport icebergs over long distances. They would partially melt, of course, but the remaining mass of ice could potentially be enough to supply a small town with fresh water for a whole year.

SINKING OF THE TITANIC

In 1912, the largest ship in the world at the time sank after striking an iceberg in the North Atlantic Ocean. 712 people survived, but more than 1,500 passengers lost their lives.

What lives in our oceans?

Water is home to many different living organisms. Seas and oceans, rivers and lakes are inhabited not only by fish, but also by mammals, reptiles, mollusks, crustaceans, corals . . . There is a vast variety of aquatic creatures, including more than 30,000 species of fish alone, and scientists continue to discover new species every year.

FISH

MAMMALS: dolphins, whales, seals, walruses, and others.

MOLLUSKS: octopuses, squids, mussels, and others,

Most marine life is found in the upper level of the ocean, referred to as the sunlight zone. This area extends from the surface to about 200 meters (about 650 feet) deep, even in the most crystal clear waters. Below this, in the ocean's extreme depths where light cannot penetrate, the water is dark and cold, with little oxygen and a great deal of pressure.

Some deep-sea dwellers can give off light—to lure their prey or to scare off predators. They are called bioluminescent animals.

REPTILES: sea turtles, sea snakes, and others.

The tiniest aquatic organisms are called plankton—bacteria, algae, protozoa, larvae, small crustaceans, fish eggs, and young fish. Plankton is a crucial source of food for many animals, including whales, the biggest animals on the planet.

CRUSTACEANS: shrimp, crabs, crayfish, lobsters, and others.

ECHINODERMS: sea urchins, starfish, and others.

JELLYFISH

SPONGES

CORALS look like fantastical, colorful trees and whimsical flowers, but corals are not plants—they are invertebrate animals.

What's on the water's surface?

There are other aquatic dwellers that wouldn't exist without rivers, lakes, seas, and oceans: boats and ships. These range from huge cruise ships and cargo ships to tug boats, yachts, ferries, and sailboats, down to small watercraft like kayaks and canoes.

Container Ship

Fishing Vessel

Tug boat

Cruise Ship

Naval Ship

Sailboat

What's on the Shore?

Since ancient times, people have settled along the shores of oceans, lakes, and rivers because they provided a steady supply of fish as well as water for drinking, washing, and watering crops. Rivers could also be used for transportation, providing access to seas and oceans and opening up possibilities for trading with other countries and discovering new lands. Most of the world's major cities are located on the shorelines of oceans and rivers for these reasons.

As of 2018, nine of the world's ten most-populated cities were located near bodies of water. The fifth-most-populated, Mexico City, was built along Lake Texcoco, but the Spanish drained its waters—creating many of the city's pollution and water supply struggles.

How powerful is water?

Water is one of the renewable sources of energy, along with sun and wind.

There is a famous proverb—"Dripping water hollows out stone"—that dates back to the writings of the ancient Roman poet Ovid. Ever since the earliest times, people have noticed the incredible power of water. Water shapes our planet, forming plains by wearing away dirt and rock from higher land, cutting river channels through mountains, and depositing sediment to make deltas and beaches.

People in ancient Rome and other civilizations learned to harness the power of water. They used water mills to grind grain into flour, and then later for tasks ranging from cutting wood and marble to making paper, leather, and woolen cloth. At the end of the nineteenth century, the first hydroelectric power plants were built, allowing the power generated by falling water to be transformed into electricity.

what are tides?

High tides and low tides are caused by the gravitational pull of the moon. As the Earth rotates, the moon's gravity pulls on different parts of our planet, generating tidal force. This force causes water to bulge out on the sides closest and farthest from the moon. These bulges of water are high tides. When you're not in one of the bulges, you experience a low tide. Since high tide and low tide fall about six hours apart, areas along the coastline experience two high tides and two low tides each day.

In the second half of the twentieth century, people started to harness the energy of tides by installing tidal electric power plants along seashores.

Hydroelectric power plants are usually built on large rivers, with a dam to hold back water and control its release.

Nearly enclosed seas, like the Black Sea, for example, have a small tidal range—you might barely notice the difference between high and low tide. But in some areas along the open ocean, tides can change the height of the water by as much as 15 meters (50 feet).

What causes flooding?

While some regions of our planet don't have enough water, others may have too much of it. Rivers and lakes sometimes overflow their banks and flood fields, towns, and even cities.

Flooding in the spring is most often caused by rapidly melting snow and ice: frozen land prevents melting snow from seeping into the ground, and ice jams prevent water from running downstream. Flooding in summer and fall is mainly caused by heavy rainfall, which typically happens during thunderstorms, hurricanes, or typhoons.

Sometimes flooding is caused by tsunamis—huge waves that crash onto the ocean's shore after an earthquake. The powerful rushing water from a tsunami can sweep away cars and destroy buildings, bridges, roads, and water supply systems.

What is life without water?

There are places on our planet where water is scarce: deserts. For example, in some parts of the Atacama Desert in Chile, it only rains an average of once every ten years.

Deserts may be dry, but they aren't necessarily hot. The McMurdo Dry Valleys in Antarctica are the driest places on Earth. There hasn't been any precipitation there for several million years.

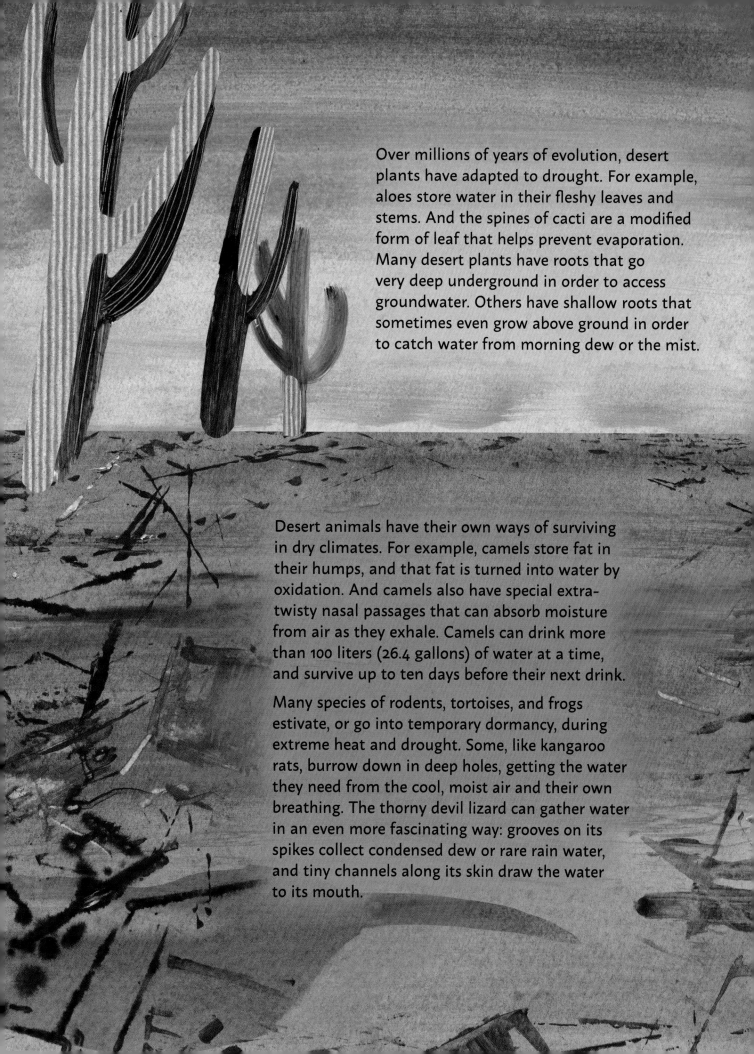

Over millions of years of evolution, desert plants have adapted to drought. For example, aloes store water in their fleshy leaves and stems. And the spines of cacti are a modified form of leaf that helps prevent evaporation. Many desert plants have roots that go very deep underground in order to access groundwater. Others have shallow roots that sometimes even grow above ground in order to catch water from morning dew or the mist.

Desert animals have their own ways of surviving in dry climates. For example, camels store fat in their humps, and that fat is turned into water by oxidation. And camels also have special extra-twisty nasal passages that can absorb moisture from air as they exhale. Camels can drink more than 100 liters (26.4 gallons) of water at a time, and survive up to ten days before their next drink.

Many species of rodents, tortoises, and frogs estivate, or go into temporary dormancy, during extreme heat and drought. Some, like kangaroo rats, burrow down in deep holes, getting the water they need from the cool, moist air and their own breathing. The thorny devil lizard can gather water in an even more fascinating way: grooves on its spikes collect condensed dew or rare rain water, and tiny channels along its skin draw the water to its mouth.

How did people get water in ancient times?

RUSSIAN WATER WELL

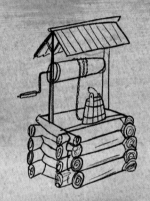

EGYPTIAN SHADUF, or WELL SWEEP

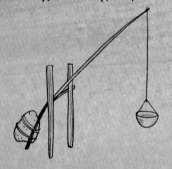

Where do you get water if there are no rivers, streams, or springs nearby? Ever since ancient times, people have noticed that if you dig a deep hole, it will fill with groundwater. This is how the first wells were made. They were lined with stones or wood to prevent collapse.

However, what is even more convenient than a single well is a water supply system—one of the greatest inventions in human history. The first simple water supply systems were built around 4000 BCE in Mesopotamia (a historic region in Western Asia), with the first sewer systems built sometime after.

The ancient Roman plumbing systems, called aqueducts, were remarkable achievements. Aqueducts channeled water from springs and rivers to cities—to supply numerous bath houses, toilets, city fountains, private residences, and gardens with water. Pipes made of stone, clay, concrete, and lead were placed at a gradual slope so that water from the source could flow downhill to its destination. Most of the time, the pipes were placed underground, but when it was necessary to cross a ravine, a deep valley, or a river, the ancient Romans constructed arch bridges.

Roman achievements were largely forgotten in the Middle Ages. In medieval European cities, people got their water from wells and rivers. Human waste was emptied into the streets, and from there it would contaminate the groundwater and other water sources. It took some time to discover the connection between this contamination and the disease epidemics that ravaged communities during those times. Only in the second half of the nineteenth century did Europeans start to build centralized systems for water supply and sewage.

One of the Roman aqueducts, built before the Common Era, is still functioning to this day, bringing water to some of the fountains of the Italian capital. It is called Acqua Vergine.

Where does the water in your tea come from?

A tea kettle! And where does the water in your tea kettle come from? A faucet. And where does that water come from? A water pipe. And where does the water in your pipes come from?

Tap water—the water we get through our faucets—usually comes from groundwater, rivers, or lakes. But first it is sent to a treatment facility to be processed and sanitized.

In areas with no access to a centralized water supply system, water is pumped up from underground wells.

The first step is to mechanically filter out any waste, plants, or animals. Then water is passed through finer sand and charcoal filters. After that, water is disinfected with ozone, sodium hypochlorite (an inorganic chemical compound), or ultraviolet light. Sometimes fluoride is added to help protect our teeth.

And finally, the water is pumped through pipes, into our homes and apartments, and even all the way to the top floors of the tallest buildings.

Used tap water drains into a sewer system and goes to a wastewater treatment plant, where it is processed and made safe to be returned back to either our drinking water supply or our local bodies of water.

What about water in cities?

Most apartments, houses, cafes, and offices have water faucets. The average person uses about 200 liters (almost 53 gallons) a day to bathe, cook, and wash clothes. We need water to produce every single thing that surrounds us. It takes up to 8,000 liters (2,113 gallons) to make a single pair of jeans, and 1,000 liters (264 gallons) to produce one kilogram (2.2 pounds) of wheat.

People living in dry regions collect rainwater and desalinate (remove salt from) seawater.

But sometimes water is wasted. A faucet can use ten liters (2.6 gallons) of water per minute. Imagine how much water you can conserve if you turn off the water while you brush your teeth, make sure your faucet doesn't drip, and regularly check to make sure your plumbing is in good shape. By doing this, you can conserve both water and the electricity used by pumps and sewage treatment plants.

Nearly a quarter of the world's population has to save each and every drop of water, especially fresh and drinkable water. Some of the most water-stressed regions are located in India, Africa, and the Middle East.

Water: inside and outside?

Around two-thirds of the human body is made up of water.

The younger you are, the more water your body contains. Body water content decreases with age.

Water transports nutrients to cells and removes wastes from cells. It regulates body temperature.

A person can survive only a few days without water.

The average person should aim to drink around 44 ml of water per kilogram of body weight each day, or two-thirds of an ounce per each pound of body weight. So, for example, a person who is 68 kg (150 lbs) should be drinking about 3 liters (100 oz) of water per day.

If you're feeling tired, sleepy, or having a headache, it's possible that your body hasn't gotten enough water. This is called dehydration.

You need to drink more water on a hot day or after physical exercise to prevent dehydration.

The first
ceramic bathtub was
discovered by archaeologists in India.
It dates back to 3000 BCE. And the first shower
was invented in ancient Greece.

Water is not only important inside the body for function and survival, it is also the foundation of personal hygiene. But this hasn't always been the case. Medieval Europeans, for example, rarely bathed. With no water supply systems, bathing was a demanding task and was considered to be a sign of softness. In the seventeenth and eighteenth centuries, many Europeans stopped bathing altogether. Doctors at the time believed that infections entered humans through widened pores after a bath.

Swimming wasn't popular either. Most Europeans couldn't swim and often drowned. To keep people safe, England even passed a law in the sixteenth century, prohibiting entering the water.

However, in Eastern Europe, people enjoyed swimming and regularly went to banyas, a kind of sauna or steam bath.

Of course, in modern times, swimming is an enjoyable activity for many people. Competitive swimming has been an Olympic sport since the first modern Olympic Games in 1896. As of the 2020 Olympics, the United States has earned the highest number of Olympic swimming medals, followed by Australia, the former nation of East Germany, Hungary, and Japan.

The word *banya* comes from the Greek *balaneion*, meaning bath. Greek priests described baths as a place for cleaning and healing the body.

What do humans think about water's mysteries?

POSEIDON
is the god of the sea
in ancient Greece.

SOBEK
is the god who
controlled the waters
of the Nile River in
ancient Egypt.

PEREPLUT
is the god of the
sea and seafaring in
Slavic mythology.

ATLAHUA
is the god of water
in Aztec mythology.

GONGGONG
is a water god in
ancient Chinese
mythology.

SUIJIN
is the Shinto god of
water in Japanese
mythology.

Many people in the ancient world believed that all acts of nature—and all the oceans, seas, rivers, and lakes—were controlled by gods and mythical creatures. They offered these gods gifts and sacrifices. They asked for rain for a good harvest, for a good catch on fishing trips, for a safe journey and calm waters for seafarers. Wrathful gods, they believed, could send storms or floods, or even drag a person to their underwater realms.

Mysterious deep seas attracted the brave, those people who were not afraid of the gods' wrath or of the unexplored depths. Humans who were bold enough to explore the oceans were rewarded for their curiosity—as in the case of divers who would swim to depths to look for oysters that contained precious pearls.

Soon enough, people started coming up with inventions to aid diving. The ancient Greek philosopher Aristotle mentioned in his works a prototype of a diving bell—an upside-down vessel that one could use to descend to the bottom of the sea. Diving bells would later be used to help search for sunken treasures or repair ships.

Deep sea diving is not easy and full of danger. Lack of oxygen, high water pressure, cold temperatures, and poor visibility— only real heroes can thrive in such conditions.

Later still came other inventions—diving suits, scuba gear, bathyscaphes—that allowed humans to explore underwater with almost no limitations.

The ocean is the largest unexplored place on Earth.

SCUBA

A "Self-Contained Underwater Breathing Apparatus" allows humans to explore up to 40 meters (131 feet) underwater.

BATHYSCAPHE

A submersible vessel used to explore the deep sea, the bathyscaphe was first invented in the mid-twentieth century. It allowed people, for the first time, to descend to the deepest location on Earth: the Challenger Deep, in the Pacific Ocean's Mariana Trench—a depth of nearly 11,000 meters (36,000 feet, or 6.82 miles).

How can we protect our planet's water?

Despite its enormous size and incredible power, the global ocean is profoundly affected by human activity. It can be damaged by oil spills that happen during oil extraction and transportation, by the illegal dumping of waste, by the excessive use of chemical fertilizers, by untreated sewage discharged into seas and oceans, by plastic pollution, and by global climate change.

One of the biggest problems is microplastics— extremely small pieces of plastic debris from car tire dust, plastic bags and packaging, microbeads that are often used in detergents and cosmetics, and many other sources. Microplastics enter water bodies through wastewater. Algae grows on floating plastic, and marine animals mistake it for food. Microplastics have been found in fish, mammals, and humans. They concentrate in our bodies and release harmful toxins.

Microplastics have even been found in clean, high-quality drinking water in every part of the world.

What can you do to protect nature and yourself?

- Use as little disposable packaging as possible.

- Recycle.

- Buy only things that you really need and that will last for years.

- Use eco-friendly detergents.

- Choose products made of cloth, glass, or paper instead of plastic.

OLGA FADEEVA is the author and illustrator of *Wind: Discovering Air in Motion*
(Eerdmans) and many other books for children. In a starred review, *Kirkus* called
Wind "thoroughly engaging...masterful in both design and imagery." Olga's art
has been honored in Italy, China, and her home country of Russia. Follow Olga
on Instagram @olgafadeeva_illustrations.

LENA TRAER is a Russian- and English-language translator with a focus on
books for children and young adults. She has translated *Wind: Discovering Air in
Motion* and *On the Edge of the World* (both Eerdmans) into English and has also
translated a variety of picture books and scientific materials into Russian. Born
and raised in Siberia, Russia, Lena now lives in San Francisco.

Text and illustrations © 2022 Olga Fadeeva
Originally published in Russia by Rech as *Вода*

Translation rights arranged through Syllabes Agency, France.
English-language translation © 2024 Lena Traer

First published in the United States in 2024
by Eerdmans Books for Young Readers,
an imprint of Wm. B. Eerdmans Publishing Co.
Grand Rapids, Michigan

www.eerdmans.com/youngreaders

33 32 31 30 29 28 27 26 25 24   1 2 3 4 5 6 7 8 9 10

ISBN 978-0-8028- 5622-7

A catalog record of this book is available from the Library of Congress.

Illustrations created with acrylic paint and water

To illustrate this book, the author generously
sprinkled, dripped, and thinned acrylic paints with
water. Approximately 10 liters (2.6 gallons) of water
were used to create the art for this book.

Eerdmans Books for Young Readers would like
to thank Jill Holz (B.S. Geology and Geophysics,
M.Ed., and National Geographic Certified Educator)
for sharing her scientific expertise for the English-
language edition of this book.

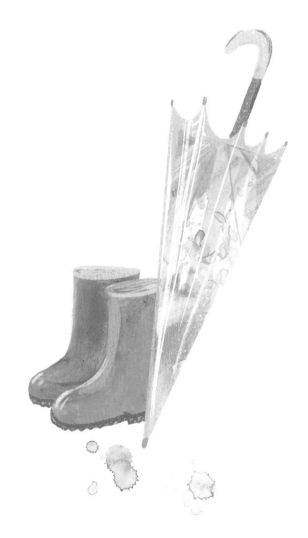

Winter temperatures in the Faroe Islands (near Denmark) are almost always above 0°C (32°F), while in Oymyakon, Russia—located at approximately the same latitude—the average high winter temperature is -45°C (-49°F). This difference is due to the influence of the warm Gulf Stream waters that flow around the Faroes.

Plants absorb water from the soil using their roots, and release most of that water into the air as water vapor from their leaves. This process is called transpiration. For example, a birch tree releases up to 400 liters (106 gallons) of water as vapor on a hot day.

It takes about 140 liters (37 gallons) of water to grow and process the beans to brew one cup of coffee.

140

The longest rain shower (with measurable rain) ever recorded was on the island of Maui, in 1939–1940. It lasted for 331 consecutive days!

Ice has different temperatures in different parts of the world. The coldest ice is in Antarctica.